PERFECT TIMING

How Isaac Murphy Became One of the World's Greatest Jockeys

BY Patsi B. Trollinger · paintings by Jerome Lagarrigue

VIKING

Much of the information for this book was gleaned from primary sources held by the Keeneland Library and the archives of the Kentucky Derby Museum. The author is grateful to staff members at each location for their assistance. Words of appreciation also go to Mary Beth Garriott and Connie Klimke of the Centre College library for answering endless questions, and to Susan Dickinson, Jerrie Oughton, and Catherine Frank for believing that the book was possible.

VIKING
Published by Penguin Group
Penguin Young Readers Group, 345 Hudson Street, New York, New York 10014, U.S.A.
Penguin Group (Canada), 90 Eglinton Avenue East, Suite 700, Toronto, Ontario, Canada M4P 2Y3 (a division of Pearson Penguin Canada Inc.)
Penguin Books Ltd, 80 Strand, London WC2R 0RL, England
Penguin Ireland, 25 St Stephen's Green, Dublin 2, Ireland (a division of Penguin Books Ltd)
Penguin Group (Australia), 250 Camberwell Road, Camberwell, Victoria 3124, Australia (a division of Pearson Australia Group Pty Ltd)
Penguin Books India Pvt Ltd, 11 Community Centre, Panchsheel Park, New Delhi – 110 017, India
Penguin Group (NZ), Cnr Airborne and Rosedale Roads, Albany, Auckland 1310, New Zealand (a division of Pearson New Zealand Ltd)
Penguin Books (South Africa) (Pty) Ltd, 24 Sturdee Avenue, Rosebank, Johannesburg 2196, South Africa

Penguin Books Ltd, Registered Offices: 80 Strand, London WC2R 0RL, England

First published in 2006 by Viking, a division of Penguin Young Readers Group

1 3 5 7 9 10 8 6 4 2

Text copyright © Patsi B. Trollinger, 2006
Illustrations copyright © Jerome Lagarrigue, 2006
All rights reserved

LIBRARY OF CONGRESS CATALOGING-IN-PUBLICATION DATA
Trollinger, Patsi B.
Perfect timing : how Isaac Murphy became one of the world's greatest jockeys / by Patsi B. Trollinger ; illustrations by Jerome Lagarrigue.
p. cm.
ISBN 0-670-06083-6 (hardcover)
1. Murphy, Isaac Burns, 1861-1896—Juvenile literature. 2. African American jockeys—Biography—Juvenile literature. 3. Jockeys—United States—Biography—Juvenile literature. 4. Horse racing—United States—History—Juvenile literature. I. Lagarrigue, Jerome, ill. II. Title.
SF336.M784T76 2006
798.40092—dc22
2005033855

Manufactured in China
Set in Janson
Book design by Kelley McIntyre

For Thelma Gray Barnes
and in memory of George W. Barnes
—P.B.T.

In loving memory of my grandmother
Virginia "Nana" Barlow
—J.L.

Isaac walked quickly through the streets of Lexington, carrying a large basket as if it weighed nothing at all. He was short for a boy of twelve, but strong. His arms had grown used to the heavy work he did for his mother's laundry business: carrying water, setting up washtubs, delivering finished loads of laundry. His grandparents had been slaves, and now Isaac was free, but Kentucky had very few schools for black students. He spent every day working with his mother.

On that spring day in 1873, Isaac made a delivery to the Owings house at the perfect time. Mr. Owings owned a stable of racehorses, and he needed to hire some new jockeys. The strong boy behind the laundry basket was just the right size for riding. Mr. Owings asked a question: Would Isaac like to learn how to ride a Thoroughbred?

The answer was yes. So early the next morning, Isaac tried to ride a volcano. Not a real mountain of fire, but a horse. Isaac had seen plenty of elegant Thoroughbreds, and he expected to ride a prince of a horse. But what did the men bring out to the paddock? A nervous young animal named Volcano. Isaac tried his best to ride, but the colt bucked, reared high, and dumped him to the ground. First day, first ride—nothing like he had imagined. Isaac was still wiping dust from his eyes when the men asked him to try again. Sore but determined, Isaac climbed back on the horse. This time, he stayed on.

With that successful ride, Isaac earned a place in jockey school. He wouldn't sit at a desk with a book, though. In this school every classroom was a stable and every lesson was a horse. It was a place where Isaac could strengthen his muscles and his mind. One man was his teacher, boss, and friend—Eli Jordan, the trainer. Eli's job was to teach Thoroughbreds and jockeys how to win races. Inside the barn, Eli explained how to feed and groom the horses. Outside on the practice track, he used one word more than any other: pace.

Isaac soon figured out that pace was a mixture of speed, strategy, and time. A jockey with perfect pace knew when to let the horse run full tilt down the track and when to save energy for a final burst of speed at the finish line.

Eli's lessons about pace were difficult. Isaac had to memorize how fast every horse could run and notice things that made each horse unique. The bay stallion hit top speed when he was leading other horses. The brown filly was just the opposite. She liked to chase other horses and pass them. If Isaac raced on the bay, he could set a fast pace all the way. On the filly, he might start slow, then finish with a final burst of speed.

Some of Isaac's best lessons came at coffee time, when the older jockeys sat on bales of hay swapping stories. One man described a racetrack with a dangerous low spot at the quarter-mile mark. Another man bragged about urging a lazy horse to a muddy victory in a rainstorm. During two years of jockey school, Isaac listened and remembered. Finally, he was ready to race.

On the morning of his first race, Isaac carefully buttoned the bright yellow shirt Eli brought to him. The silk racing shirt and matching cap announced that Isaac was a real jockey.

At the starting line, he became part of a patchwork of colors, each representing a different stable. Isaac focused on one small piece of red—the starter's flag.

It happened suddenly. The starter lowered the flag, and all the horses lunged forward, so crowded that they bumped one another. A cloud of dust sprayed Isaac's head and stung his eyes. Chunks of dirt flew up and hit his legs. He was supposed to think about timing and tick off each second in his head. But his counting disappeared into the noise of pounding hooves.

Before Isaac had time to think clearly, before he could set a pace, the race was over. He didn't win.

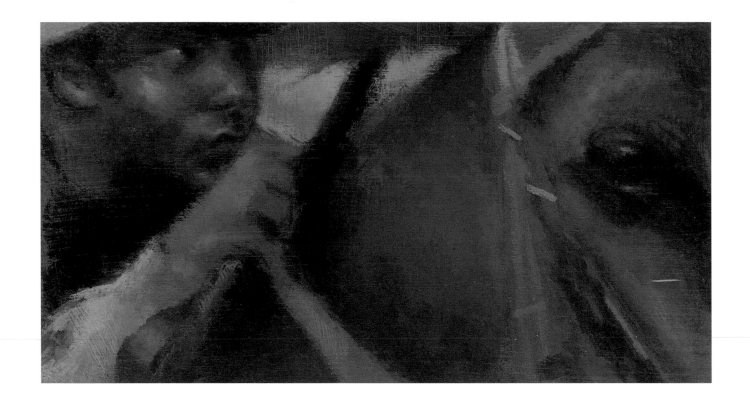

By the time he wore the yellow silks again, Isaac had learned how to concentrate. There was noise all around him, but Isaac had ears only for the strong, steady breathing of his horse. From the moment the race began, the seconds ticked clearly in his head. *Fifty-eight*, he told himself at the half-mile mark. *One hundred fourteen*, as the one-mile mark slipped by. On the final stretch, the dust and noise faded away. Isaac and his horse were headed for victory! His timing had been perfect.

Other wins followed. Suddenly, horse owners all over the country wanted Isaac to ride for them. He began racing at tracks in New York, Florida, and Missouri. No matter where he rode or what color silk he wore, Isaac kept on winning.

Isaac became famous, but it didn't change who he was. He had rules for himself that were firm: no cheating, no fighting, no swearing. And he rode every race, large or small, as if it was the most important one of his life.

By the spring of 1882, Isaac was very busy. But when he met a beautiful girl named Lucy, he still had time for love. They were married that year, and some of Isaac's friends wondered if he might quit racing. Jockeys were often away from home, and sometimes the job was dangerous. Lucy understood those things and supported Isaac's love of the track. In his first year as a married man, he won thirty-three races.

During the next few years, Isaac won a lot of important races. He won the American Derby four times and the Latonia Derby five times, earning some of the nation's highest prize money. By 1890, some people believed he was unbeatable. After he won several races that year on a colt named Salvator, there was talk that Isaac might guide the big horse to a world's record by running a mile in less than one hundred seconds.

Most people were certain that no horse could beat Salvator, but Isaac knew there was one. Tenny was small for a Thoroughbred, yet he could run like the wind. When the two horses finally met in a race, Tenny challenged Salvator every step of the way. Even so, Isaac guided the bigger horse to a victory. Tenny's owner was furious. He demanded a match race, a special event for just two horses and two riders.

Forty thousand people overflowed the grandstand on Coney Island that June day. The two jockeys could not have been more different. Isaac believed that a jockey should look dignified, so he stayed cool and calm in the saddle. Snapper Garrison, the other jockey, had the riding style of a wild man. He kept his body folded low and he constantly flailed the reins.

At the drop of the flag, Snapper forced Tenny to bolt from the starting line. Moments later, Isaac moved Salvator out front. Seconds ticked away, and Snapper pushed Tenny past them again. It was the last quarter mile when Isaac and Salvator regained the lead. The crowd went wild.

Near the end of the race, Isaac heard the determined hoofbeats of Tenny. He knew that the small horse was cutting Salvator's lead and pulling even. The time had come for Isaac to make his final move. He leaned forward, encouraging Salvator. The big horse strained harder and, with a final tremendous stride, won the race. Isaac and Salvator not only beat Tenny, they tied the world's record.

That win gave Isaac a reputation as the best jockey in the history of horseracing. His fame grew even more when he won the Kentucky Derby three times. Now when men and boys gossiped in the horse barn over steaming cups of coffee, they talked about Isaac Murphy.

Isaac continued to win races for six years after the Salvator-Tenny match, but as he got older, the racing began to affect his health. Every spring Isaac had to go on a diet to lose weight. A jockey wasn't supposed to weigh more than 110 pounds during the racing season. Anything extra would put a strain on the horse. Sometimes after a winter of rest and good food, Isaac had to lose 20 pounds or more. He was so determined to continue riding that he tried to lose weight too quickly. One cold biscuit for breakfast and a cup of hot coffee for lunch—that was all he would eat. After he fainted one day in the horse barn, a doctor warned him to be more careful. Isaac listened to the advice, but found it hard to change old habits.

In the fall of 1895, Isaac was hired to ride a horse named Tupto, who often finished last. With Isaac in the saddle, Tupto won. That turned out to be Isaac's final race. The following spring, he went on another crash diet and became so weak that he contracted pneumonia.

Isaac died February 12, 1896. He was only thirty-five. Two days later, more than five hundred people filled the streets of Lexington for Isaac's funeral procession. Many of the grandest bouquets of flowers came from jockeys who had ridden against him.

In the years since Isaac's death, the racing community has continued to honor him. He was one of the first people inducted into the Jockey Hall of Fame in Maryland. Tracks in Florida and Illinois have named races for him. He is the only jockey buried on the grounds of the Kentucky Horse Park, and he still holds the record for the highest percentage of racing wins ever (44 percent of all his races). Isaac Murphy is remembered as a brilliant rider whose timing was always perfect.

Isaac Murphy's Life—A Time Line

- 1861 – Born near Lexington, Kentucky.
- 1873 – Makes first attempt to ride, on a yearling named Volcano.
- 1874 – Achieves first win, on a filly named Glentina.
- 1884 – Wins first Kentucky Derby victory, on an ill-tempered horse named Buchanan. The horse threw Isaac before the start of the race, but he returned to the saddle and rode to victory.
- 1884 – Wins three major races in one week: the Kentucky Derby, the Kentucky Oaks, and the Clark Stakes. No other jockey has ever achieved this.
- 1890 – Ties world-record time for one mile in match race on Salvator.
- 1891 – Sets a record by winning the Kentucky Derby for a third time.
- 1896 – Dies in Lexington, Kentucky. Given a hero's funeral.
- 1967 – Grave is moved to an honorary location in Kentucky Horse Park.

Author's Note

Throughout his life, Isaac Murphy seemed to have a perfect sense of timing—his career even came at a perfect time.

If Isaac had been born twenty years earlier, he would have raced as a slave rider. Every penny of his prize money would have belonged to his master. If Isaac had been born twenty years later, he might never have ridden at all. By that time, white jockeys had become more common, and some of them did not want to ride with black jockeys. These white riders began to force black men out of the sport by causing accidents. Many black jockeys quit. Others moved to Europe, where racetracks welcomed them. With each passing year, there were fewer black riders in the United States. By 1922, there were no black jockeys in the Kentucky Derby.

But for the two decades that followed the Civil War—the years when Isaac rode—horse owners were willing to hire black riders. During those years, black men and white men raced side by side.

Today, people in the United States have more enlightened ideas and laws about race relations. Black jockeys do not dominate horseracing as they did in the 1800s, but riders of all backgrounds are welcome at racetracks. If Isaac came back to ride again, he would see Hispanics, Asians, and women on horseback, as well as blacks. And he would find that people still talk about the great Isaac Murphy, the jockey with perfect timing.